My First Science Bo

DAY TURNS INTO NIGHT

Patricia Armentrout

A Crabtree Seedlings Book

CRABTREE
Publishing Company
www.crabtreebooks.com

Table of Contents

Day

The **Sun** is rising in the sky. It is time to wake up. A new **day** has begun!

We call it daytime when the Sun is up.

Earth (our world)

The Sun shines on our **world**. Its

helps us see. It keeps us warm.

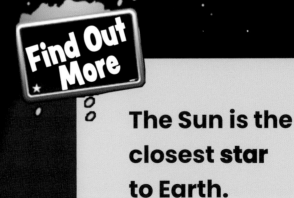

Find Out
More

The Sun is the
closest star
to Earth.

Sunlight helps plants and animals live and grow.

Look up at the sky during the day.

Can you see **clouds**, a blue sky, birds, and planes?

Sometimes you can see the **Moon** in the daytime sky.

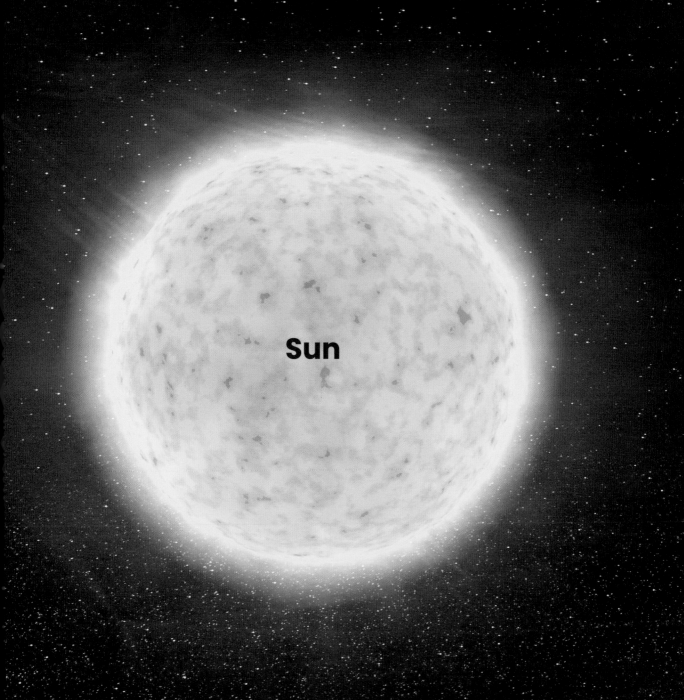

Sun

A full day lasts 24 hours. But we only see the Sun for part of the day.

Earth

daytime

nighttime

Night

Sunset is the time of day when the Sun goes down.

The sky grows dark. Daytime becomes nighttime.

What can you see in the **night** sky?

Can you see the Moon?

What shape is it?

Can you see stars or the blinking lights on planes as they fly across the sky?

Nighttime makes us sleepy.
It is time for bed, but that's okay.
Tomorrow the Sun will rise again.

GLOSSARY

clouds (KLOUDZ): Clouds are white or gray groups of water droplets that float in the air.

day (DAY): A day is 24-hour period; the period between sunrise and sunset when it is light.

Moon (MOON): The Moon is a natural satellite that moves around a planet.

night (NYTE): Night is the part of the day without sunlight.

star (STAR): A star is a ball of burning gas in outer space that gives off light.

Sun (SUHN): The Sun is the closest star to Earth.

sunset (SUHN set): Sunset is the period of the day when we lose sunlight and it becomes dark.

world (WERLD): The world is planet Earth.

INDEX

School-to-Home Support for Caregivers and Teachers

This book helps children grow by letting them practice reading. Here are a few guiding questions to help the reader build his or her comprehension skills. Possible answers appear here in red.

Before Reading

- **What do I think this book is about?** *I think this book is about nighttime. I think this book is about when it gets dark.*

- **What do I want to learn about this topic?** *I want to learn how it gets dark at night. I want to learn why the Sun goes away at night.*

During Reading

- **I wonder why...** *I wonder why sunlight helps plants grow. I wonder why the sky is blue.*

- **What have I learned so far?** *I have learned that sometimes you can see the Moon in the daytime. I have learned that a full day lasts for 24 hours.*

After Reading

- **What details did I learn about this topic?** *I have learned that sunset is the time of day when the Sun goes down. I have learned that the Sun is the closest star to Earth.*

- **Read the book again and look for the glossary words.** *I see the word **Sun** on page 2, and the word **Moon** on page 10. The other glossary words are on page 23.*

Library and Archives Canada Cataloguing in Publication

Title: Day turns into night / Patricia Armentrout.
Names: Armentrout, Patricia, 1960- author.
Description: Series statement: My first science books | "A Crabtree seedlings book". | Includes index.
Identifiers: Canadiana (print) 2021020382X |
    Canadiana (ebook) 20210203838 |
    ISBN 9781427159441 (hardcover) |
    ISBN 9781427159526 (softcover) |
    ISBN 9781427159496 (HTML) |
    ISBN 9781427160171 (EPUB) |
    ISBN 9781427160140 (read-along ebook)
Subjects: LCSH: Day—Juvenile literature. | LCSH: Night—Juvenile literature. |
    LCSH: Earth (Planet)—Rotation—Juvenile literature.
Classification: LCC QB633 .A76 2022 | DDC j525/.35—dc23

Library of Congress Cataloging-in-Publication Data

Available at the Library of Congress

Crabtree Publishing Company
www.crabtreebooks.com   1–800–387–7650

Written by Patricia Armentrout
Print coordinator: Katherine Berti

Print book version produced jointly with Blue Door Education in 2022

Printed in the U.S.A./062021/CG20210401

Published in the United States
Crabtree Publishing
347 Fifth Ave.
Suite 1402-145
New York, NY 10016

Published in Canada
Crabtree Publishing
616 Welland Ave.
St. Catharines, Ontario
L2M 5V6